W9-CCR-382

To: grandma

From: Rene

Why: Because I ♡ You!

and I love this movie thanks
to you.

White Christmas

RUTLEDGE HILL PRESS®

Nashville, Tennessee

A DIVISION OF THOMAS NELSON, INC.

www.ThomasNelson.com

Copyright © 2004 Paramount Pictures Corp. All Rights Reserved.
Material on snow copyright © 2004 by Rutledge Hill Press.
Oscar® is the registered trademark and service mark of the
Academy of Motion Picture Arts and Sciences.

All rights reserved.
No portion of this book may be reproduced, stored in a
retrieval system, or transmitted in any form or by any means —
electronic, mechanical, photocopy, recording, or any other — except for
brief quotations in printed reviews, without prior permission of the publisher.

Published by Rutledge Hill Press, a Division of Thomas Nelson, Inc.,
P.O. Box 141000, Nashville, Tennessee 37214.

Photo credits: Images on page 18, 39, and 49 licensed through Getty Images.
Page 42 licensed through Corbis Images. Page 52 licensed through Photonica.
All other images © Paramount Picture Corp.

The following sources were used in compiling this book: IrvingBerlin.com;
Girl Singer: An Autobiography by Rosemary Clooney (New York: Doubleday, 1999);
Call Me Lucky by Bing Crosby as told to Pete Martin (New York: Da Capo Press, 1993);
White Christmas: The Story of an American Song by Jody Rosen (New York: Scribner, 2002).

Cover & text design by Bruce Gore / Gore Studio, Inc., Nashville, Tennessee

ISBN 1-4016-0192-8

Printed in the United States of America

04 05 06 07 08 — 5 4 3 2 1

Introduction

AT ITS most basic level, the movie *White Christmas* is about friendship, it is about sacrifice, it is about love, and it is about family.

The song "White Christmas" was first performed by Bing Crosby on December 25, 1941, during the darkest days of World War II. Throughout the war, Bing's singing of a white Christmas, of snow-covered trees, of children, and of sleigh bells often brought tears to the eyes of soldiers far away from home.

The movie *White Christmas* was first released in 1954, and even today it helps us forget how busy we are and lets us remember a childhood when snow didn't mean traffic problems and wondering what to do with the kids when school is called off. *White Christmas* reminds us of the romance and the nostalgia of a time when a big snowfall meant building snowmen and making snow angels. It reminds us of making

snow cream and having the biggest fort in our neighborhood. It makes us think about sleigh rides and snowball fights and winter nights by the fire. But most important, *White Christmas* makes us think about what's really meaningful in life.

As you look through this book that celebrates the fiftieth anniversary of one of the world's favorite films, we hope you will be reminded of your favorite Christmases and want to share those memories with the ones you love.

The Song Behind the Film

"White Christmas" was already one of the most popular songs of the decade before the film *White Christmas* was released. In 1941 Irving Berlin was asked to write a song about each major holiday for the movie *Holiday Inn* starring Bing Crosby and Fred Astaire. And although Berlin found writing a song about Christmas the most difficult of all, when Bing Crosby first heard "White Christmas," he assured Berlin that he had a winner. Many of the other songs in *Holiday Inn* have been forgotten, but "White Christmas" remains popular more than sixty years later. It won an Oscar® for best original song in 1942 and became the best-selling Christmas song of all time.

White Christmas

SILENT NIGHT • ADESTE FIDELES • WHITE CHRISTMAS • GOD REST YE MERRY GENTLEMEN •
FAITH OF OUR FATHERS • I'LL BE HOME FOR CHRISTMAS • JINGLE BELLS (With The Andrews Sisters) •
SANTA CLAUS IS COMIN' TO TOWN (With The Andrews Sisters) • SILVER BELLS
(With Carole Richards) • IT'S BEGINNING TO LOOK LIKE CHRISTMAS • CHRISTMAS IN KILLARNEY •
MELE KALIKIMAKA (MERRY CHRISTMAS) (With The Andrews Sisters)

A Career- and Era-Defining Song

"White Christmas" hit the pop charts every year in the decade prior to the 1954 release of the movie *White Christmas*. Anytime Bing Crosby performed the song for soldiers during World War II, it had a powerful emotional effect, and by the time the film was released, the song "White Christmas" had sold more than nine million copies. In fact, by that time, the song had already appeared in three other motion pictures. Today "White Christmas" is the best-selling Christmas record of all time.

White Christmas Cast

Bob Wallace	**BING CROSBY**
Phil Davis	**DANNY KAYE**
Betty	**ROSEMARY CLOONEY**
Judy	**VERA-ELLEN**
General Waverly	**DEAN JAGGER**
Emma	**MARY WICKES**
Susan	**ANNE WHITFIELD**

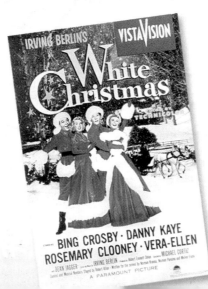

A Christmas Storyline

White Christmas spins the romantically humorous tale of two army buddies, Bob Wallace and Phil Davis (Bing Crosby and Danny Kaye), who become a topnotch musical comedy team after the war and eventually produce their own Broadway hits. They become involved with a sister act — Betty and Judy (Rosemary Clooney and Vera-Ellen) — and the foursome proceeds to Vermont to spend a white Christmas.

Bob and Phil discover that the inn at which they are quartered is owned by General Waverly (Dean Jagger), their former commanding officer who is now retired. Waverly's investment is in danger because of unseasonably warm weather and lack of snow. Winter snow enthusiasts are staying away in droves.

To promote business over the Yule holidays, the boys bring their new show to the inn for a pre-Broadway warm-up. They also take advantage of the occasion and stage a reunion of the general's wartime division.

Romantic complications ensue, but all ends happily Christmas Eve when the big show is playing and the long-awaited snow is falling outside.

Irving Berlin's **White Christmas**

COPYRIGHT MCMLIV BY PARAMOUNT PICTURES CORPORATION

ALL RIGHTS RESERVED

Paramount Pictures Corporation

BERLIN'S BELOVED 'WHITE CHRISTM
FINDS NEW FAME IN FABULOUS F

VISTAVISION

"WHITE CHRISTMAS" TEAMS FOR THE FIRST TIME THE TWO MEN GENERALLY REGARDED AS THE DECADE'S FINEST ENTERTAINERS, BING CROSBY AND DANNY KAYE

IRVING BERLIN'S
White Christmas
IN VISTAVISION

Starring BING CROSBY · DANNY KAYE · ROSEMARY CLOONEY
VERA-ELLEN
Color by TECHNICOLOR
A PARAMOUNT PICTURE

Snow-It-All

Is it ever too cold to snow?

No!

As long as there
is some source of
moisture in the air,
it can snow.

Although
most larger
snowfalls do occur
when the air is
warmer near
the ground,
it is in fact never
too cold to snow.

Bing Crosby

HARRY LILLIS CROSBY got his nickname "Bing" from the leading character in his favorite comic strip, *The Bingville Bungle*. Born and raised in the state of Washington, Bing tried the college route, but music was his true love. He left home at the age of twenty-two to go to Los Angeles, where he found work on the vaudeville circuit. In 1931 he recorded his first solo hit record, "I Surrender Dear." In 1932 he made his first big film, *The Big Broadcast*. Between 1944 and 1948, Bing was the most popular box office draw in the United States. An Oscar® winner for *Going My Way*, he also starred in the very successful "Road" movies with Bob Hope and Dorothy Lamour. In the seventies, his "Little Drummer Boy" duet with David Bowie introduced Crosby to a whole new generation. Bing was an avid golfer and the founder of the Bing Crosby Pro-Am golf tournament. He died in 1977.

Did You Know?

Bing Crosby...

Made more studio recordings than any other singer in history.

※

Made the most popular Christmas record ever, "White Christmas,"
the only single to make American pop charts twenty times,
every year but one between 1942 and 1952.

※

Scored the most number one hits ever—thirty-eight—compared with
twenty-four by the Beatles and eighteen by Elvis Presley.

※

Received a platinum record in 1960 as First Citizen
of the Record Industry for having sold two hundred million discs,
a number that doubled by 1980.

※

Was nominated for an Academy Award for best actor
three times and won for *Going My Way*.

※

Financed and popularized the development of
audiotape, revolutionizing the recording industry.

Snow-It-All

Is it true
that no two
snowflakes
are alike?

Yes!

Snowflakes are all
unique because they are
made up of snow crystals
that combine in
different ways.

White Christmas NOTES

"How about a dame called Rosemary Clooney? Sings a good song—and is purportedly personable."

— BING CROSBY
(from a letter written to Paramount Pictures during the time *White Christmas* was in development)

Rosemary Clooney

Born in Maysville, Kentucky, ROSEMARY CLOONEY began performing at the age of thirteen with her sister Betty. In 1949 she signed a record contract with Mitch Miller, and in 1951 Rosemary had her first hit song, "Come On'a My House." Later hits included "Hey There," "Mambo Italiano," and "This Ole House." The mother of five children, Clooney was married to Oscar®-winning actor Jose Ferrer and later to dancer Dante DiPaolo. She was the aunt of George Clooney and the sister of AMC movie host Nick Clooney.

Despite numerous challenges, Clooney never gave up. She was awarded a lifetime achievement Grammy just a few months before her death in 2002.

"The picture was a wonderful medley of show-biz and holiday spirit, with sleigh bells and saxophones, red satin Santa suits with white fur muffs. It was an absolute joy to sit by the fire in that Vermont lodge and sing "Count Your Blessings" with Bing. Singing together came as naturally to each of us as breathing."

— ROSEMARY CLOONEY

Snow-It-All

How to make snow cream...

COMBINE:

- 2   quarts of milk
- 2   cups of sugar
- 1   tablespoon of vanilla

Once mixed, add snow to absorb the liquid mixture
(probably 3–4 quarts of snow).

Serve immediately, and freeze leftovers—it is snow after all.

Irving Berlin

Born Israel Beilin in a Russian Jewish *shtetl* in 1888, he died as Irving Berlin in his adopted homeland of New York, New York, USA, in 1989. He was a songwriter, performer, theater owner, music publisher, soldier, and patriot, and when he wrote the lyric, "God bless America / Land that I love," Irving Berlin meant every word.

He wrote over 1,200 songs, including "White Christmas," "Easter Parade," "Always," "Blue Skies," "Cheek to Cheek," "There's No Business Like Show Business," "Alexander's Ragtime Band," and "God Bless America." He wrote the scores to more than a dozen Broadway musicals, including *Annie Get Your Gun* and *Call Me Madam*, and he provided songs for dozens of Hollywood movie musicals. Among his many awards and accolades were the Academy Award for "White Christmas," a special Tony Award, three Presidential medals, and commemoration on a United States postage stamp.

"Irving Berlin has no place in American music," the composer Jerome Kern once said. "He *is* American music."

Snow-It-All

What Does It Mean?

SNOWFLAKE
A cluster of ice crystals that falls from a cloud.

SNOW FLURRIES
Snow that falls for short periods of time with changes
in intensity and usually results in little or no accumulation.

SNOW SQUALL
A brief but intense snowfall that greatly reduces visibility
and is accompanied by strong winds.

BLIZZARD
Winds of at least thirty-five miles per hour coupled with snowfall that reduces
visibility to less than one-quarter of a mile for a period of at least three hours.

Danny Kaye

Born in Brooklyn, New York, in 1913, DANNY KAYE was the son of an immigrant Russian tailor. After dropping out of high school, he worked for a radio station and later as a comedian in the Catskills. In 1939 Kaye made his Broadway debut in *The Straw Hat Review*.

The show-stopping performance that put Danny Kaye on the map was in *Lady in the Dark*—he belted out the song "Tchaikovsky," in which he reeled off the names of fifty-four Russian composers in thirty-eight seconds.

In addition to his role in *White Christmas*, Kaye also dazzled audiences with his performances in *The Secret Life of Walter Mitty*, *The Inspector General*, *Hans Christian Anderson*, and *The Court Jester*.

In 1954 Danny Kaye began working with UNICEF, the United Nations Children's Fund, and traveling to developing countries to entertain children. His association with UNICEF lasted until the time of his death in 1987.

Kaye was also a guest conductor for numerous symphony orchestras around the world, raising tens of millions of dollars for symphony musicians' pension funds.

Danny Kaye was the winner of two Academy Awards. In 1954 he was awarded a special Oscar® for his unique talents and for his service to the Academy, the motion picture industry, and the American people. In 1981 Kaye was given the Jean Hersholt Humanitarian Award.

Snow-It-All

How to build a perfect snowman...

Your snow should be firm and not too fluffy.
If the snow sticks together easily, then you are ready to begin.

Roll three balls of snow. The first one should be about three feet in diameter,
the next about two feet, and the smallest about one foot.

Place the two-foot snowball on top of the three-foot snowball. Then put
the one-foot snowball on top of the two-foot snowball.

Complete your creation using buttons, rocks, coal, or any other small
round objects to form the mouth and eyes. Add a carrot to form the nose.
Be creative and add other objects—hats or caps, scarves, and other items
of clothing—to make your snowman stand out from the crowd.
Don't forget to add sticks or something else to simulate arms.

Michael Curtiz

One of the most successful directors in film history, MICHAEL CURTIZ ran away from his home in Budapest at the age of seventeen to join the circus. His stint in the circus led to work as an actor in the Hungarian theater before he began his career as a director.

In addition to *White Christmas*, Curtiz also directed *The Adventures of Robin Hood*, *Angels with Dirty Faces*, *Yankee Doodle Dandy*, *Mildred Pierce*, *Night and Day*, *Life with Father*, and *Casablanca*, for which he received an Academy Award.

Curtiz died in 1962, one year after making his final film, *The Comancheros*.

Snow-It-All

How to make a snow angel...

Lie down in the snow with your legs together
and arms straight out. Move your legs apart back and
forth to form the base of the angel. To form the
wings, move your arms up and down as
if you were trying to fly.

Get up, brush yourself off, and enjoy
the results of your efforts!

Vera-Ellen

VERA-ELLEN was born in Cincinnati in 1921. She began dancing at the age of ten and became one of the youngest Rockettes ever. She also danced on Broadway before making her 1945 film debut in *Wonder Man* with Danny Kaye, her costar in *White Christmas*.

Some of Vera-Ellen's best-known films are *On the Town*, *Slaughter on Tenth Avenue*, *Happy Go Lovely*, and *The Belle of New York*. Many have said Vera-Ellen is the only female dancer who is the peer of both Fred Astaire and Gene Kelly.

White Christmas FACTS

The scene in which Bing Crosby and Danny Kaye impersonate the Haynes sisters was originally done as a gag by the two during rehearsals, surprising the director Michael Curtiz and others. The cameras were rolling and the scene went over so well it was added to the picture.

Snow-It-All

How to make the perfect snowball...

Use good wet snow, which is best when the temperature is in the neighborhood of ten to thirty degrees. It will be wetter and stickier at these temperatures.

Form a ball that fits in your hand. You are officially allowed to make the first snowball of each season without gloves on, but all others must be made with gloves on or people will question your sanity and common sense.

Find a friend or sibling who has it coming.

Let it go!

Dean Jagger

Born and raised on a farm in Ohio, DEAN JAGGER became a teacher after graduating from Wabash College in Indiana. But he was bitten by the acting bug and soon quit teaching to study his craft. It looked like the right move, as he soon began getting roles in theater, vaudeville, and radio.

The consummate character actor, Jagger won an Academy Award in 1949 for his performance in *Twelve O'Clock High*. He appeared in other films of note, including *Elmer Gantry*, *Brigham Young*, *The Robe*, *King Creole*, and *Bad Day at Black Rock*. Jagger died in 1991.

Snow-It-All

How to make a snow candle...

This craft, courtesy of Mother Nature,
looks great lining a driveway or in front of a house.

Make approximately twenty-five snowballs. Each snowball
should be the size of a tennis ball. Make a circle in the snow using
about a dozen of the snowballs. This is your base.

Now take a candle and place it in a shallow yet sturdy container.
The candle should be no more than six inches in height, but larger than a
votive or a tea light candle. Take about eight of the remaining snowballs and
make a second circle by placing them on top of the first circle. In order to
do this, you will have to begin a slant that will create an angle. Be sure
to leave several open spaces that will allow the candle to glow.
Follow this with another circle of four snowballs.

Finally, light the candle and then place the
one remaining snowball on top.

Use leftover snowballs to exact revenge on anyone
who made fun of your beautiful project.

OPENING
XMAS EVE
BOB
WALLACE & PHIL
DAVIS
with
THE NEW YORK CAST
in
THEIR NEW MUSICAL
"Playing Around"
Music by
BOB WALLACE
Lyrics by
PHIL DAVIS

TOP TALENT, MUSIC, AMAZING VISTAVISION SPARK IRVING BERLIN'S "WHITE CHRISTMAS"

IRVING BERLIN'S
White Christmas
PRESENTED THROUGH VISTAVISION MOTION PICTURE HIGH-FIDELITY
ING   DANNY   ROSEMARY   VERA-
OSBY · KAYE · CLOONEY · ELLEN
Color by TECHNICOLOR

N JAGGER · Lyrics and Music by IRVING BERLIN · ROBERT EMMETT DOLAN · Directed by MICHAEL CURTIZ
Produced by
Written for the screen by
NORMAN KRASNA, NORMAN PANAMA and MELVIN FRANK · A PARAMOUNT PICTURE
Suggested by a play by
Robert Allen

To Bob
From Betty

Mary Wickes

With a film career that lasted almost sixty years, MARY WICKES had a voice, a face, and a style that made audiences love her and laugh with her. From her first big role in *The Man Who Came to Dinner* in 1941, to her later roles in films such as *Sister Act*, *Postcards from the Edge*, and *Little Women*, and her voice talent in Disney's *Hunchback of Notre Dame*, Wickes set the standard for playing nosy neighbors, smart-alecky housekeepers, gruff but lovable nuns, and old-maid aunts.

Wickes was the model for Cruella DeVille in *101 Dalmatians*, and the original Mary Poppins in the television series of the same name. She died in 1995, just days after finishing her work on *The Hunchback of Notre Dame*.

Snow-It-All

How to get an up-close and personal look at a snowflake...

Everyone knows that if you catch a snowflake in your hand, it will melt almost immediately. The secret to getting a good look at one of nature's miracles is to catch the snow on a frozen piece of black fabric—preferably velvet.

Cut a small piece of velvet and lightly glue it to a piece of cardboard. Put the velvet in the freezer for at least an hour.

Take the velvet outside, and catch several snowflakes on it. You will have just a few moments to enjoy the beauty of the snowflakes under a magnifying glass.

White Christmas FACTS

Bing Crosby's version of the song "White Christmas" marked the end of the Vietnam War. In 1975 Americans who remained in Saigon were told to listen for a cue on the radio to begin their evacuation as the North Vietnamese surrounded the city. The radio cue was the announcement that the temperature was "105 degrees and rising," followed by Bing Crosby singing "White Christmas." When "White Christmas" began to play, there was a mad scramble for the United States embassy, where helicopters were waiting to take U.S. citizens to safety.

"It's 105 degrees and rising..."

Snow-It-All

Will you have a white Christmas this year?

Here are the chances of having at least one inch of snow on December 25...

ALABAMA
Huntsville · 3%

ALASKA
Juneau · 100%

ARIZONA
Flagstaff · 56%

ARKANSAS
Little Rock · 3%

CALIFORNIA
Los Angeles · 0%

COLORADO
Denver · 50%

CONNECTICUT
Hartford · 57%

DELAWARE
Wilmington · 13%

DISTRICT OF COLUMBIA
13%

FLORIDA
Miami · 0%

GEORGIA
Savannah · 0%

HAWAII
Maui · 0%

IDAHO
Boise · 30%

ILLINOIS
Chicago · 40%

INDIANA
South Bend · 67%

IOWA
Des Moines · 50%

KANSAS
Wichita · 23%

KENTUCKY
Louisville · 13%

LOUISIANA New Orleans · 0%	**NEW HAMPSHIRE** Concord · 87%	**SOUTH CAROLINA** Charleston · 3%
MAINE Caribou · 97%	**NEW JERSEY** Atlantic City · 7%	**SOUTH DAKOTA** Pierre · 47%
MARYLAND Salisbury · 14%	**NEW MEXICO** Albuquerque · 3%	**TENNESSEE** Nashville · 13%
MASSACHUSETTS Boston · 23%	**NEW YORK** New York · 10%	**TEXAS** Amarillo · 7%
MICHIGAN Lansing · 73%	**NORTH CAROLINA** Greensboro · 10%	**UTAH** Salt Lake City · 53%
MINNESOTA International Falls · 100%	**NORTH DAKOTA** Bismarck · 87%	**VERMONT** Montpelier · 93%
MISSISSIPPI Jackson · 3%	**OHIO** Cleveland · 50%	**VIRGINIA** Roanoke · 17%
MISSOURI St. Louis · 23%	**OKLAHOMA** Tulsa · 7%	**WASHINGTON** Stampede Pass · 100%
MONTANA Butte · 87%	**OREGON** Redmond · 20%	**WEST VIRGINIA** Morgantown · 31%
NEBRASKA Omaha · 44%	**PENNSYLVANIA** Allentown · 30%	**WISCONSIN** Milwaukee · 60%
NEVADA Winnemucca · 37%	**RHODE ISLAND** 37%	**WYOMING** Laramie · 48%

Over the years, many have invoked White Christmas as evidence that the 1950s were a simpler time. I'm not sure I agree with that. The 1950s certainly were not simpler for me. There was the Korean War, the McCarthy hearings, Brown vs. the Board of Education, and the birth of rock & roll, among other things.

What we see on the screen is not, of course, the way we really were. It was the way we hoped the world would see us. Perhaps most of all, it was the way we wanted to be.

White Christmas wasn't just Bing's picture, after all. It was mine, too, and Mr. Berlin's and Danny's and Vera's and Dean's—and yours. There we are, bigger than life, frozen forever in our moment.

The intervening years have not all been easy or kind, but I confess there is a part of me that still believes it all. Sentimental songs, boy-meets-girl stories, happy endings—all of it.

If White Christmas has any enduring legacy for generations to come, perhaps that's it. A stubborn optimism that looks ahead in hope, not back in anger.

Merry Christmas,
ROSEMARY CLOONEY